I0568980

I FORGIVE MYSELF FOR

FORGETTING MYSELF

SHATIERA MYESHA PORTE'E

For permission requests, write to the publisher, addressed "Attention: Permissions Coordinator," 205 N. Michigan Avenue, Suite #810, Chicago, IL 60601. 13th & Joan books may be purchased for educational, business or sales promotional use. For information, please email the Sales Department at sales@13thandjoan.com.

Printed in the U. S. A.

First Printing, May 2022.

Library of Congress Cataloging-in-Publication Data has been applied for.

ISBN: 978-1-953156-61-7

Black Frail Girl
Whipped by fear
Body beaten
Unable to stand
Her mind screams
Independence no longer a choice
A slave of torture
Where to run?
Her mind races again
Overthinking becomes tiresome
Life, a private failure.

TODAY IS THE DAY
I FORGIVE MYSELF
FOR
FORGETTING MYSELF.

This book is dedicated to you!

You is not only you, but it's also me and anyone else who will find strength in being vulnerable.

Apologize to yourself now and say with me,

"I FORGIVE MYSELF FOR FORGETTING MYSELF."

You are an amazing soul who has made a powerful decision to be BRAVE!

You have made a powerful choice to begin a new journey. You are now on the path of putting yourself first.

This book is dedicated to empower and support your thoughts, feelings, questions, and guide you when your words seem to be lost.

It allows you to flood these pages as you dive deeper within yourself.

The powerful choice is that you believe in yourself!

*Now forgive yourself because
you will no longer forget about you.*

The #1 thing to remember is that

No Experience is Required. ☺

A beginner starts somewhere, gets lost on the journey, feels the feeling and moves on. *The best part is taking the first step.*

Contents

Preface

I remember the first day when I was in my room feeling the lowest of lows. I was journaling my feelings of sadness. How I felt unloved and how I didn't feel beautiful. I had tears coming down my face. I didn't even take a shower that day. I felt like my legs were so numb from laying in the bed, balled into a circle, feeling like I couldn't get up. I didn't have any purpose. The lack of faith in me and my feelings of unworthiness were overwhelming.

I felt so unsure of myself. I felt defeated. I wanted someone to hug me. I wanted someone to love me. I wanted someone to tell me everything was going to be alright. I began to feel like I gave up on myself, that I wasn't good enough, that nobody loved me, and that I was failing. I wasn't making anybody proud. And I realized I needed help.

I no longer felt all the support I had growing up. I felt lost. The pages of my journal that day were about depression, low self esteem, lack of self-love, and tons of insecurities I had as a young woman.

I was battling my most private demons within myself. My thoughts had no one to turn to. So I began journaling every day, sometimes even two to three times a day. I realized that it was helping me release some pain, some memories from childhood, and from what I was feeling from unspoken words of fear that I had never told a soul. It felt good.

So I kept writing and I kept writing and eventually it became a practice for me. It became my first step in healing.

Journaling became a part of a routine for me to get down on paper the things that were killing me inside. I realized that I have a story and that my story could be somebody else's story. So I continued to write and write.

But then I started second guessing myself. Should I be sharing these things? Will anyone care? I went from writing every day to watching days pass by without me looking in my journal at all. I would keep it closed and buried in my drawer next to the bed under piles and piles of paper. Not sure if I wanted to continue, but the reality is, I had a burning desire to keep writing my story.

I would hear my notebook calling to me, "come write, come write, free yourself. Get these words on paper." So I stopped running from it and I said, "okay, let me grab that notebook." There were days where I was crying. I was afraid to open the notebook. I was afraid to keep writing. I was afraid of what was going to come out. I felt as if I was suppressing so many different things. There were feelings and experiences I had that I had never shared with anyone and didn't even want to think about, but one day something pulled me to that drawer. I opened that first drawer next to my bed. I took out all those papers. I sat on the bed, pulled the covers over me. I propped the pillow behind my back and I started to write, and I started to like what I was writing.

It felt good.

I felt free.

I felt inspired.

I felt encouraged every week. I would take a day and I would begin reading what I wrote. And it would make me very emotional to say, "wow, I didn't know I had all of that in me," and I didn't stop there. I revisited the idea of wanting to share my story with others.

My Life...
My Process...
My Victory...

I was always looking for a community where I felt I belonged. Where I could get support, you know like a sisterhood. Somewhere where I didn't feel out of place. The more I searched I began to feel more insecure, awkward, and alone. I was craving mentorship, connections, and a place called home with "my girls." I was helping others but was still looking for the same sacred space I was providing for everyone else. Listen, I can admit that I was hanging on to some friendships and relationships that could have hit the road a long time ago. We've all been there.

Eventually my notebook became my best friend. A consistent place I could confide in. I knew from my writing that there was work to be done within myself. I decided it was time for self healing. I made a powerful choice that changed my life. I was on a mission to become a better version of myself.

I forgive myself for
forgetting about myself.
I forgive myself for not loving
myself the way I deserve.
I will protect my heart and
treat myself with honor,
because I know,

I AM ENOUGH!

Reader's Note

This journal is a blank canvas of pure white, no lines, no borders. When you choose to paint your canvas with colors of feelings, hues of thoughts, pastels of heart, and bold dark colors of emotions, you can break free from the things that hold you hostage. The pages of this book are meant to become your emotional masterpiece and to help you discover your voice. Allow me to take you on a journey of heart, mind, body, and soul.

Blank Pages Untouched

I write
to make peace
with pain
and hurt I cannot control

I write
to unveil shame and sin
Left naked, humbled, frightened, vulnerable.
Fill the pages.

I write
To hear my voice
lost in conversations when I speak

I write
To free my soul

Unplugged and Unjudged

I write
to honor my beauty

Complete thyself

Ignite my dreams

My journey begins

Reawakening...

"Today I choose to live my best life for the rest of my life."

— *Trenice Byers*

.

Introduction

Grandma's Orphan

A child alone
Cradled in Grandma's arms
Longing for a mother's love

A child grew into a woman who learned not to smile. At an early age, I unknowingly was preparing for my life journey, not having a clue what I would be getting myself into.

Fed by words from my mother, so powerful that I couldn't swallow.
"I should've aborted you."
These words would haunt me. An injection of loneliness, neglect, weakness, and failure. I derailed, listening to the echoes of pain in my life that I was never built to endure.

How can my very own mother look right through me and scream those exact words? Words that have pierced my soul.

Beaten by fear so that I could learn to hold my own.
Never would I count my blessings.
Never have I waved at the sun.
Never did I look at love the same again.

My empty mirror later showed visions of that same woman I have learned to take after. Holding onto anyone that caressed my heart.

During the journey of writing this book, I have truly forgiven my mother. I honor her today. I salute the survivor she has become.

No one is perfect. As a teenage mother with two kids less than a year apart, she was a child herself. Those awful words that she spoke also prepared me for my life. I thank her.

Though you have the least amount of control of how you come into the world, you have every bit of control of how you mark your destiny. As I got older, I always wanted to achieve many things. I sought out love, begged for it, and looked desperately for validation wherever I could find it. School, relationships, substance abuse, and creating alter egos, were my ways of escaping my personal problems. It helped me put my issues to the back of my mind since I refused to talk about them with anyone. I wanted to be number one in my own life and I felt like I wasn't even number one in either of my parent's lives. I became excellent at being lost within myself, all from being a child whose basic needs have never been met by her parents. My life could have ended, but as you can see here, you are reading my story so you know that I have conquered fighting for my life. I am alive today! This book is to help inspire you. Letting you know that you are not alone, you are not by yourself! I decided to use my paper and pen to share my experiences, my story. I have shared my personal stories of my relationship with life lessons and my story of inspiration and resilience of how I overcame the challenges of life and continue to pursue my dreams. This book will include affirmations and journal prompts to motivate, guide reflection, and ignite and establish self confidence. Faith and Forgiveness have been my two main tools to help me become the resilient woman I am today. Before you do anything else, let's put you first. Honor thyself and let's dive in!

"How you start your day is
how you ground your day."

Trent Shelton

PART I:

Reflect

My purpose is greater than my fears.

What is my calling?

_____

_____

_____

_____

_____

_____

_____

_____

_____

_____

Be intentional with surrounding yourself with people, places, and things that fill you up with peace. The energy you give out will be the energy you attract.

All that I need is within me.

I will conquer...

_____

_____

_____

_____

_____

_____

_____

_____

_____

_____

CHOOSE TO GROW AND STOP PLAYING SMALL.

I am proud of the person I am becoming.

I am truly grateful for...

_____

_____

_____

_____

_____

_____

_____

_____

_____

Feed your soul.

My strength is unstoppable.

My superpower is...

_____

_____

_____

_____

_____

_____

_____

_____

_____

_____

GIVE YOURSELF
PERMISSION TO RELEASE
ALL THINGS THAT
NO LONGER MATCH
YOUR WARDROBE OF
TRUE HAPPINESS.

I will win in all areas of my life.

Three ways I will empower and motivate myself...

_____

_____

_____

_____

_____

_____

_____

_____

_____

_____

Celebrate yourself everyday.

I am resilient.

I forgive myself for...

_____

_____

_____

_____

_____

_____

_____

_____

_____

_____

CANCEL ALL DOUBTS.
OPINIONS DON'T MATTER.
I choose me.

I am enough.

I will use these three resources to help me grow (my support team, therapist, professional development, etc.)...

_____

_____

_____

_____

_____

_____

_____

_____

_____

_____

If I take my cape off, who am I?
Find your superpower.

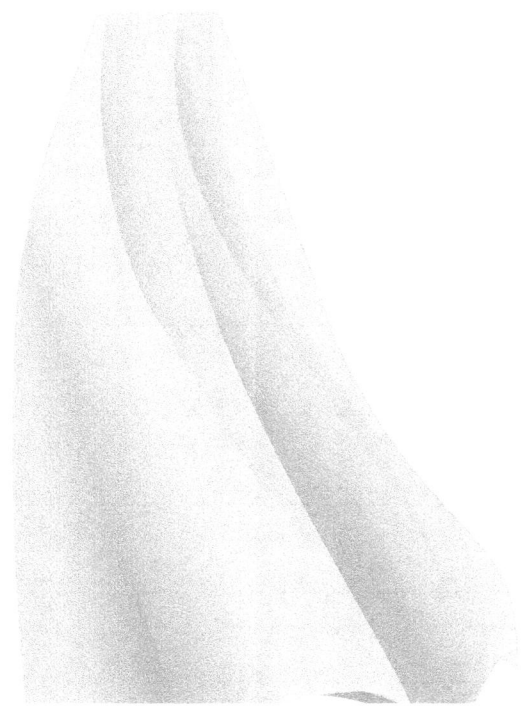

I am unapologetic.

Three things I am walking away from that no longer serve me...

_____

_____

_____

_____

_____

_____

_____

_____

_____

Take inventory of your life.

I am committed to loving myself unconditionally.

I feel most confident when I allow myself to...

_____

_____

_____

_____

_____

_____

_____

_____

_____

_____

GET RID OF ANY BAGGAGE.

I am brave.

Three things I will manifest today are...

_____

_____

_____

_____

_____

_____

_____

_____

_____

_____

PART II:

Affirm

I will do anything I put my mind to.

Today I will create...

_____

_____

_____

_____

_____

_____

_____

_____

_____

_____

Create boundaries.

I am at peace in all areas of my life.

Three things I need to make me happy...

_____

_____

_____

_____

_____

_____

_____

_____

_____

_____

COURAGE OVER COMFORT.

I am stronger everyday.

Today I am proud of...

_____

_____

_____

_____

_____

_____

_____

_____

_____

_____

Love on yourself today.

I am beautiful inside and out.

Three compliments I give myself are...

_____

_____

_____

_____

_____

_____

_____

_____

_____

_____

DREAM BIG AND GO FOR IT!

I am confident.

I will stay true to myself by...

_____

_____

_____

_____

_____

_____

_____

_____

_____

_____

CREATE POSITIVE ENERGY.

I am aligned with the vision I see for myself.

My vision is...

_____

_____

_____

_____

_____

_____

_____

_____

_____

Become your own leader.

I am disciplined and consistent.

Today I will excel at...

_____

_____

_____

_____

_____

_____

_____

_____

_____

_____

SHOW UP IN ALL AREAS OF YOUR LIFE.

I am safe and protected.

Write about one fear you are releasing today...

_____

_____

_____

_____

_____

_____

_____

_____

_____

_____

B.A.E.

"Becoming and Elevating."
I am showing up in my
life the way I show up for
others unapologetically!

My talents drive my success.

Three things that make me unique are...

_____

_____

_____

_____

_____

_____

_____

_____

_____

_____

I AM USING MY VOICE
TO REACH MY GOALS
AND GET WHAT I
WANT OUT OF LIFE.

I am fearless and I trust the universe.

Even though it scares me I am going to...

_____

_____

_____

_____

_____

_____

_____

_____

_____

_____

PART III:

Express

I am freeing myself by forgiving everyone who has hurt me.

Take a deep breath. List someone you will forgive right now and what you are forgiving them for...

_____

_____

_____

_____

_____

_____

_____

_____

_____

THE GREATER VERSION OF YOU IS READY FOR YOU.

I am blossoming.

I will show up for myself today by...

_____

_____

_____

_____

_____

_____

_____

_____

_____

_____

No more getting offended,
it's time to get inspired!

I am wealthy and prosperous in every aspect of my life.

Three areas of my life I will be successful in are...

_____

_____

_____

_____

_____

_____

_____

_____

_____

_____

WATER THE SEEDS IN YOUR LIFE SO YOU CAN GROW.

I surround myself with positive people, places, and things that help me reach my goals.

Safe places that help me grow...

_____

_____

_____

_____

_____

_____

_____

_____

_____

_____

Create a visionary
mindset
&
Find your
purpose.

I am amazing.

How can I celebrate myself today?

_____

_____

_____

_____

_____

_____

_____

_____

_____

_____

MY POWER IS IN MY VOICE.

I am healthy.

I will be mindful in making sure...

_____

_____

_____

_____

_____

_____

_____

_____

_____

CREATE INVITE-ONLY SPACES IN YOUR LIFE.

I trust myself in creating the life I desire.

How will I put myself first today?

_____

_____

_____

_____

_____

_____

_____

_____

_____

_____

My winning
season is now!

My heart is full and pure.

Today I will practice self love by...

_____

_____

_____

_____

_____

_____

_____

_____

_____

_____

I am no longer living in my head.

I am allowing myself to heal.

An accomplishment my younger self would be proud of...

_____

_____

_____

_____

_____

_____

_____

_____

_____

_____

I AM SHOWING UP AS MY WHOLE SELF EVERY DAY.

I deserve anything I desire.

The goal I intend on accomplishing today is...

_____

_____

_____

_____

_____

_____

_____

_____

_____

_____

PART IV:

Inflect

I choose to communicate effectively.

Today I command that I will...

_____

_____

_____

_____

_____

_____

_____

_____

_____

_____

TODAY I HAVE DECIDED THAT I AM SHOWING UP DIFFERENTLY IN ALL AREAS OF MY LIFE.

I will wake up bright and bold everyday.

Things that make me smile...

_____

_____

_____

_____

_____

_____

_____

_____

_____

_____

Quiet the noise that does not matter.

I am secure.

Things that win my heart...

_____

_____

_____

_____

_____

_____

_____

_____

_____

_____

_____

BE PRESENT AND LIVE IN THE MOMENT.

I am impactful.

Everyday I will commit to...

_____

_____

_____

_____

_____

_____

_____

_____

_____

_____

Create new
memories that
make you smile.

I feel full of life.

All things that give me energy...

_____

_____

_____

_____

_____

_____

_____

_____

_____

BE OPEN TO LOVE,
HAVE FAITH,
ALLOW FORGIVENESS,
FOCUS ON GROWTH.

I allow myself to flourish in
the abundance of joy.

I will be intentional today with...

_____

_____

_____

_____

_____

_____

_____

_____

_____

_____

Be mindful of where you invest your time.

I am confident in all the things I have to share with the world.

What do I need that will allow me to live my life with happiness?

_____

_____

_____

_____

_____

_____

_____

_____

_____

_____

BE YOUR AUTHENTIC SELF. EVERYTHING WILL COME ORGANICALLY.

I am daringly showing up every day in my life.

What makes me vulnerable at this moment right now?

_____

_____

_____

_____

_____

_____

_____

_____

_____

_____

Take care of your heart.

My self care comes first.

My daily self care plan will include...

_____

_____

_____

_____

_____

_____

_____

_____

_____

_____

GET RID OF WHAT IS EXPIRED IN YOUR LIFE TO BECOME A BETTER YOU!

My self acceptance has set me free.

To become a better version of myself, moving forward I will...

_____

_____

_____

_____

_____

_____

_____

_____

_____

Reflect on who you were and who you are becoming. Now affirm your worthiness and value with positivity. Express yourself and let the power of your voice dictate how you begin to move forward in your life. This is the "under construction" version of you. This is just the beginning of the inner work of awareness, self reflection, bravery, and consistency that will be needed for the next steps.

The "Under Construction" Challenge

As you are on this journey of making yourself a priority, I challenge you for the next 7 days to allow your thoughts and heart to connect with each other to create a new dialogue. The 7 Day Writing Plan allows you to set the tone for each day with daily writing goals to keep you grounded. Now that you have used the affirmations and journal prompts to guide you in creating a new positive mindset, the writing plan will help create new activities you can incorporate into your everyday routine.

The 7 Day Writing Plan

**"How you start your day is how
you ground your day."
Trent Shelton**

For the next seven days I challenge you to use writing to help you become a better version of yourself. Journaling is a form of expression that allows you to express yourself in a safe place. Each day you will read and complete a new writing prompt. The purpose of The 7 Day Writing Plan is to make daily time for your thoughts and to create the positive energy and mindset you desire.

Let's Begin.

DAY #1:
Letter To My Younger Self

I remember when I was 18 years old,
Getting ready to go to college.
I was leaving my grandmother's home,
Everybody used to laugh at me.
They used to say that when I was little
I used to be stuck to my grandmother's leg.
I would hold her leg and she would have to pry me off to separate me from her.

I was a little nervous.
I was in a relationship, you know,
and it was becoming toxic for me.
And I was just leaving my job.
I wasn't sure if I was going to go and finish college.

Years later, I became the first in my family to attend and complete college.
And the first one in my family to earn a graduate degree.

When I was 18 my mom had another child
and she was still dealing with her addiction and other things.
My grandmother was helping my mom balance everything.
And I was helping with my new baby sister.

So at that time I was thinking about dropping out of college,
just to help my grandma.
She was working two jobs and I said, you know, she needs my help.
I can't go to college.

And I was also dealing with low self-esteem and anger. I was very angry at that time and sad.

So if I had to write a letter to my younger self at that time, I would probably say...

Dear Shatiera

You have so much strength. You are beautiful.

I know you're scared to embark on this new journey but you must take the first step. You are supported, you are loved, you can do amazing things, and every step that has happened up until this point has prepared you for you to do well in college. You're going to do amazing things. Just know to use your resources and that home is not too far away.

This is your time to find your voice. It starts now.

Love,
Your biggest supporter,

Shatiera

Use the space below to write a letter to your younger self.

Dear (Your Name) ,

_____

_____

_____

_____

_____

_____

_____

_____

_____

_____

_____

Let's check in.

"How's your heart?"
~Iyana Anderson, LCSW, Well Together LLC

Before you answer, think about how your heart is really feeling. We are programmed to respond so quickly with a response that does not actually reflect what we are truly feeling. Stop saying you are good if that is not how you are actually feeling. It is okay to feel exactly what you are feeling. You have spoken, written, and thought of many memories and emotions from this book. That is a huge accomplishment and excuse me, but to be honest, some deep shit! As we continue to grow and become self aware it is important to acknowledge you and what you are feeling. All of it.

So, may I ask, how is your heart?

Inside the heart, write or draw what your heart is feeling.

Now take a deep breath. Your heart matters. Your feelings matter. You matter. Create the heart that now smiles. ☺

DAY #2:
The Circle of Reflection

Reflection Circles are a safe space for connecting with yourself through the authentic expression of your thoughts. This is a practice of mindfulness. Use the circle to write what is on your mind.

Now choose one thought and write below how you are feeling with this particular thought.

_____

_____

_____

_____

_____

_____

_____

_____

_____

_____

_____

DAY #3:
Dare to Be Brave

Create your own mantra. Your mantra will be a single sentence or a phrase you will recite every day to help guide your thoughts in a positive way.

_____

_____

_____

_____

_____

_____

_____

_____

_____

_____

DAY #4:
Practicing Gratitude

Use the table below to create a list of all the things you are grateful for.

"IF I TAKE MY CAPE OFF, WHO AM I?"

Monique Credle

DAY #5:
Mirror Exercise

Write below what you see when you look in the mirror.

_____

_____

_____

_____

_____

_____

_____

_____

_____

_____

Now look in the mirror and write about all the things you love when you look at yourself.

_____

_____

_____

_____

_____

_____

_____

_____

_____

_____

_____

_____

DAY #6:
Self-Talk

Use the quote boxes below to write positive phrases that you should speak to yourself.

DAY #7:
Final Thoughts

What have you learned about yourself after completing the The 7 Day Writing Plan?

_____

_____

_____

_____

_____

_____

_____

_____

_____

_____

What are you most proud of?

_____

_____

_____

_____

_____

_____

_____

_____

_____

_____

_____

_____

Dear Dope Soul,

Congratulations on completing the The 7 Day Writing Plan Challenge and finishing the book. Kudos to you for your hard work, discipline, and consistency. You now are on a new path of taking steps to honoring your needs, wants, desires, and goals. It takes a winner like yourself to come face to face with the deeper you. Writing can be intimidating. Don't worry about your penmanship or even trying to be the best speller. You are in control of your thoughts and feelings. Manifest in your mind, spirit, and heart all you deserve. You deserve the best.

Use this book as your safe place, your keepsake. You have now created healthy mindful thoughts. You can set the tone for yourself everyday. I understand there are times you may feel misunderstood. There will be days when obstacles may arise but those are growing pains. Use this book to cite an affirmation, journal a positive thought, recite positive self-talk, and find one thing that makes you smile. Find a safe community and even a licensed professional to support you as you continue to do your work.

Take these reminders with you. SAY IT WITH ME RIGHT NOW ALOUD,

"I AM STRONG, BRAVE, RESILIENT!"

Life is preparing you for all your blessings. Don't stop here. Hug yourself, love yourself, nurture yourself, and believe in yourself. Anything is possible.

Hashtag
#iforgivemyselfforforgettingmyself

I AM WALKING FREELY TOWARDS MY PEACE.

My healing has begun!

Join A Dope Girl Vision Movement

I would love for you to be a part of A Dope Girl Vision movement. No, it's not only for girls.

A DOPE GIRL VISION's mission is to empower others to create their own vision through self discovery, encouragement, networking, mentorship, and developing new interests that allows one to become the person they're striving to be.

A Dope Girl Vision is not only an online retail store selling products, services, or events; a Dope Girl Vision is about building up our community and the people around us, inspiring those who dare to be inspired, and giving back. A Dope Girl Vision is the heartwork of two women who saw a need not only in our homes and in the lives of our loved ones but also in our community. A Dope Girl Vision is about building a culture to create a boss mindset through our events, programs, and merchandise.

We have a host of great things we provide such as journals, notebooks, office supplies, and clothing.

Check us out and Manifest your vision today!

www.adopegirlvision.org
IG adopegirlvision

School Counselor on Wheels LLC

"Counseling beyond the classroom"

School Counselor on Wheels LLC is an education consulting company that provides student services in various organizations serving students in grades K-12. Our primary goal is to empower youth to connect, communicate and collaborate with themselves and others to build, strengthen, and promote self-love within.

School Counselor On Wheels, LLC mission is achieving student life-long success for underserved and under-resourced youth to help overcome challenges, cope with extenuating life circumstances, and reach their post-secondary goals with ongoing support. School Counselor On Wheels LLC offers programs for youth to be equipped with skills to feel good about themselves through promoting confidence, self-love, self-awareness, relationship building skills, responsible decision making so that each individual will be more connected to themselves and their communities.

School Counselor On Wheels LLC presents the option for in-person learning, virtual learning, or a combination of both that will meet and exceed your organization's counseling needs and requirements.

Please visit IG: @SchoolCounselorOnWheels
Facebook: School Counselor On Wheels, LLC
https://www.schoolcounseloronwheels.com

Acknowledgements

To my entire Porte'e and Cagle family, I love you and I wouldn't trade you for the world.

Thank you Uncle Rob for being like a father figure to me. I love you ☺

To my guardian angels:
"Nadie, Uncle Parrish-"P-Funk," Naomi, Uncle Willie, Uncle Bobby, Uncle Larry, and Uncle Alvin, thank you for looking over me. I feel your presence with me daily.

My sweet angel Nan, I wish you were here to read my first book. I can hear your voice now, "Sha-dee, I'm so proud of you." Thank you for your life teachings, making sure I was your "smart little cookie." I feel you with me everywhere I go. I will continue to make you proud. I love and miss you.

To my writing coaches Mrs. Ruby Simmons and Mr. William Cramer, we did it. I say "we" because your support, coaching, and patience has helped me get to the finish line, "The Mighty Marathon." You two encouraged me not to give up and saw me always having several books. The second book is on its way. ☺ I dedicate this book to the two of you!

Ardre Orie and team, I can't thank you all enough for all you have done that included positive self talk, Ardre Writing Retreats, and events to help new authors like me find their voice and share their stories. I am truly grateful for all of you.

To Mary and Lynette, we are the "Top three!" 2022 is the year all of us will be number one best sellers.

To all my friends, family, my spiritual accountability partner Meta Boo, and my support team, I thank you for all your support, text messages, phone calls, outings, prayers, love, laughs, and friendship. I love my circle and my tribe. Thank you for betting on me. It is only up from here. We won't stop. We deserve the best.

I am truly grateful for one of my accountability partners, Alicia Fusco. You were never too busy for me and I look up to you. You have no idea. Thank you.

Dr. Nadira Jack, in the short amount of time we have known each other, you have become not only my sister but my mentor. You're stuck with me now!

Coach By Joc, I got it together sis and it was because of your mentoring and coaching! You are a part of my awakening. I forgot about myself in so many ways and because of you I have forgiven myself. Thank you for being the vessel in my life to teach me to honor thyself and to be unapologetic about it. I love you for life.

Pastor Sarah Jakes Roberts, my first Woman Evolve Conference helped me face my fears. Thank you!

Dr. Lori, thank you for helping me become the best version of myself and for helping me "unpack my boxes." I couldn't step into this new journey without you!

To my beautiful sister Nyree, continue to shine bright. I love the amazing young woman you're becoming. I created this book for amazing souls like you to use as a resource as you conquer your life journey.

To my brother Bee, thank you for being one of my best friends and having my back no matter what. Even on my darkest days your words of encouragement and wisdom got me to write this book we have in our hands today and put myself first. I will forever be grateful. Thank you for allowing me to see my worth. I love you!

To the best person that has come into my life, my son Kymier! You're the best thing that has happened to me. As your mother you've helped me grow as a person and you have accepted me and loved me unconditionally. Your kindness and good heart make me proud. You have helped me become a better Mom. I look up to you. Thank you for making sure I wrote my book.

To my dearest Keeka, I honor you today. Not only as my mother but as my role model. Your resilience can not be matched. As a teenage mother you chose my siblings and I, despite your circumstances. For that reason alone I love you more than anything. I am proud of you and I just want you to know that I am proud to have you as my mother.

Lastly, there is no Shatiera without "Mom" - my best friend. Without hesitation as my grandmother, you stepped into the huge shoes of being my mother :-) You always saw in me things I couldn't or was afraid to see in myself. I always looked up to you and hoped to embody the class and wisdom you have as my grandmother. Thank you for your unconditional love Mom. I couldn't do this thing called life without you. We did it :)

About the Author

Shatiera Porte'e, MA, LAC, NCC

As a child, Shatiera experienced first hand feeling alone, low self-esteem and lacked self-love. Shatiera has been challenged with several adversities and struggles throughout her life. However, her life lessons have helped mold her into a stronger woman. Shatiera knows the importance and value of honoring one's self and now is empowering others by sharing her own story as well as the tools and resources she used to overcome challenges, unhealthy relationships, while finding herself. Shatiera wanted to create a space to help kids who feel alone to feel supported and empowered. She always knew what she wanted; inspiring to help people one day. During her academic school years, she fell in love with the study of the mind and behavior.

Shatiera has been working in the mental health field for almost two decades and as a school counselor for nearly one. She has successfully rolled out and optimized more than a dozen programs, initiatives, and projects for businesses and communities. Shatiera has extensive experience in various counseling capacities, corrections, residential treatment facilities with adolescents, long term care facilities, emergency crisis and psychiatric screening services, homeless youth, support needs of individuals with intellectual and developmental disabilities, and substance abuse treatment centers.

Shatiera launched School Counselor On Wheels, LLC. She designs programs to support students with necessary skills for success, to overcome challenges, and to cope with traumatic experiences and circumstances. Shatiera enjoys traveling abroad especially for community outreach including teaching at a school in Haiti and volunteering at an orphanage in Morocco.

Shatiera is a co-founder of A Dope Girl Vision, LLC where she conducts seminars promoting self-discovery and empowerment to participants to cultivate visions of the person they are destined to become. Armed with a plethora of education and experience, Shatiera is passionate about bridging the gap between accessibility to counseling services and those who could need it the most. Shatiera resides in New Jersey with her son and loves spending time with family. She enjoys cooking, creating new recipes, finding new places to travel, and becoming an international foodie. She also likes to dance while listening to her favorite selections of music. Shatiera is working diligently to one day establish her own nonprofit organization to help young ladies manifest their desired dreams.

www.ingramcontent.com/pod-product-compliance
Lightning Source LLC
Chambersburg PA
CBHW071007120626
46546CB00003B/965